# Differences Make Us Special!

Celebrating Differences

Lela Lawson

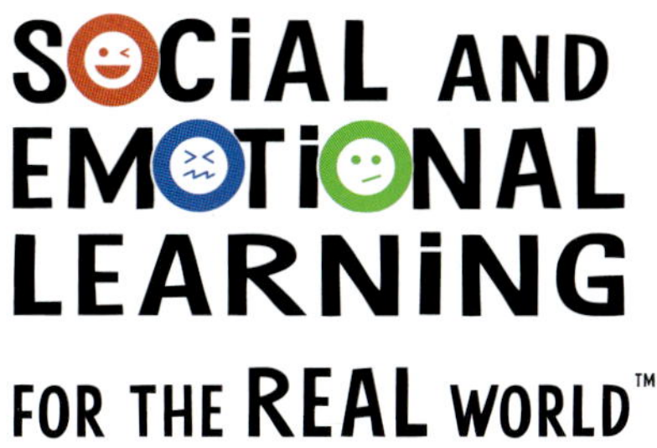

No two people are the same.
We are all very different!

Some people are mean to others. That is not fair.

You can celebrate differences. Keep an open mind!

People have different skin colors. Every color should be celebrated!

People have different abilities.
Some use a wheelchair.
You can all work together.

People believe different things.
You can listen to their ideas.

People come from different places. You can learn about their home.

People wear different clothes.
Treat everyone with kindness.

You can be friends with people who are different.
Treat them with respect.

Get to know many different people. Celebrate your differences!

# Words to Know

clothes

skin

wheelchair